Don't Know How To Say It

Don't Know How To Say It

Copyright © 2022 Pamela Brown

All rights reserved.

Printed in the United States of America. No part of this book may be used or reproduced in any manner whatsoever without the written permission except in the case of brief quotations embodied in critical articles or reviews.

ISBN: 978-1-7367637-6-6

Cover art by Paper and Sage

Don't Know How To Say It

Pamela Brown

Also by Pamela Brown

<u>Poetry</u>

How It Happened: Poems

All Through the Years: Poems

<u>Novel</u>

I Know the Plans

For every introvert

who struggles to speak their mind

I don't know how to say these things.

I stumble when I start.

My tongue gets tied; my mouth gets dry.

My words get lost inside.

I can't speak from my heart.

My thoughts get jumbled when I try

Cause I don't know how to say this…

Don't Know How To Say It

Part I – Hope

Part II – Family

Part III – Faith

Part IV – Grief

Part V – Love

Part VI – Peace

Part VII - Reflections

Hope

Fireflies

Fireflies are a part of me now,

since I learned to breathe.

Scuffling for a break,

just a break in the waves,

a flashlight in the thick dark night.

Swallowing my hope,

and inevitably my pride.

Swallowing these deep wounds.

Then, just a break,

just a break in the night,

illuminating me.

And I swallow the light,

breathing hope into this life.

Radioactive

I've got glitter in my heart,

glitter on my shoes.

Sparkle when I walk-

radioactive shining through.

This glimmer of hope,

illuminating everything I do.

Glitter all around me,

sprinkling gold over the blues.

On the Verge of Truly Breathing

Should I quell this desire,

this ripening feeling,

this powerful force inside my heart?

It's burning out of control.

My wings have grown and now I'm finally free.

Don't tell me I must destroy it.

Better Days

Better looking days

washing over me.

Silent years, silent strife -

a distant memory.

Emotional Embellishment

On the cusp of bravery;

weak in despair – nevermore.

Watch how this hope does grow!

Towering greatness,

moving on from the bleak.

Gifts of Platitudes

Oh, don't bother now.

There's peace inside of me.

There's purpose dwelling deep,

sparking its flame,

lighting a torch of hope

behind my eyes.

So don't bring gifts of platitudes

to lift my spirit,

uplift my heart.

Your belated tropes aren't needed here,

for I found my own sense of pride.

A Fire Inside

Everyday, every long and lonely day
there's a fire in her eyes.
Every door, every locked and guarded door
has something waiting on the other side.
And does she knock and step gently inside,
whispering words so kind?
If she did, she'd never get through those doors.
Never daunted, she kicks them open and cries,
"Here I am. Here I stand.
Let me have my every wish and demand."

And as others stand at every locked door,
wishing they could get in,
they look longingly at her cruising through,
making all of her dreams come true.
As they are too shy to try
anything quite so bold,
she passes by in all her gold.
And she says,

"Here I am. Here I stand.
Let me have my every wish and demand."

As time is drifting, others can see.
Dreams are passing; time is lapsing.
Now others can see.

Everything, every unimportant thing
has led up to what they've had.
Every time life has fallen short
of the hope they've been fed.
A fire burns in their eyes;
a light illuminates their zeal.
Now they won't be denied of the joy
they were promised all their years.
They scream. They cry.
"Here we are. Here we stand.
Let us have our every wish and demand."

Everyday, ever long and lonely day
there's a fire burning bright.

The Fight

This passion never stops

impressing on my thoughts,

invading and raiding every moment I relax.

The complacency effaced

by unrequited love

can't be assuaged by another placating word.

But there's an honest hope

to the promise spoke,

and I will cling for the moment

to the meager chances that I have.

And I will fling my tears

back through the weary years.

I've thrown away the blueprints

of the wreckage in my soul.

And I might be making a big mistake

placing all my hope inside,

placing all my eggs in one glass jar.

Fate would say

don't woo this way,

don't place your chips on a bet that hasn't been tried.

But I am on a trajectory

that's been undefined,

destined for a certain course while still on this side.

And it could all end up for ruin,

but so could everything for that matter.

There's nothing that is certain but life and death and taxes.

How to Handle Daylight?

How to handle midnight?

Bottled up and stored

inside its hollow core,

infiltrating body, mind, and soul.

Trembling forces

barging in on the space

of one already weakened.

So distraught, so destroyed.

How to handle twilight?

Eclipsing space and sky.

Darkness clinging to the land,

denying light its rightful claim.

Hope just beyond all reach-

visible yet denied,

frustrating the soul,

paralyzing the mind.

How to handle daylight?

Arising on the side,

birthing over the sea.

The east alit with heavenly fire,

bridging soft and slowly,

pushing night into its place.

Covering earth and man and beast.

Covering the heart inside of me.

Things I Have to Remind Myself

Slight progression is still progression,

is it not?

I may be crawling inch by inch

through broken glass,

but at least I'm moving forward.

Family

Holiday

Warm sighs.

Warm welcomes.

Warm hugs.

A handshake here.

A handshake there.

The new members enter,

and the vultures swoop down for their prey-

circling and criticizing,

remembering and revising the memories.

More food, more wine, more lies.

Here you are daughter.

Don't trust your grandmother.

Why thank you son.

Who does your uncle think he is?

Hearty laughter proceeds.

Warm sighs.

Warm welcomes.

Warm hugs.

Father

My heart contusion,

broken illusions,

swept under the rug

for others to believe.

Twisted star,

you're not who others think you are.

Not again. Not again.

You're not my friend.

My sweet good-bye;

sweet lullaby.

Deceitful mister,

you're nothing but a lie.

I followed you all the way,

but now I see your broken side.

Not again. Not again.

You're not my friend.

I Don't Care

Why do I worry about the wrath of others?

Why do I worry about the disappointment of others?

Why do I worry about the pain of others?

Why do I worry about the heartache of others?

Why do I worry about hurting others

when they don't care about hurting me?

We All Rise

We all rise,

building each other

brick-by-brick,

creating this castle of resilience.

Although we stumble,

the mortar unsure,

trouble rising and flowing

like floodwater amid the storm,

rushing against us with fury and flame.

We do not shudder,

though pressed to our knees.

We do not shake,

though crippled and bleeding.

But we stand tall-

shoulder to shoulder,

brick to brick,

building each other

until we all rise.

Faith

Idle Man

It's unsettling, isn't it?

Somewhat overwhelming,

as the ticket master says,

while his palms greedily devour

a week's pay.

Unsettling to know

how these things stand,

how matters rest in another's hands.

A dark sigh and a deep stare

can conquer wee demands.

Best to wait for conquerable hands,

lest we all lose out in the end.

All-powerful, all-conquerable,

unsurpassable hands.

Conflagration

Not by my own decision,

not by power of my own,

You've come into my heart,

and resuscitated my world.

Until My Heart is Free

Not gonna worry.

Not gonna cry.

Not gonna mope.

Not gonna complain.

Not gonna be lonely.

Not gonna long.

Not gonna be ungrateful.

Not gonna hypothesize.

Not gonna dwell.

Not gonna struggle against You anymore.

This Cosmic Realm

Underneath the shimmering stars,

gazing at the heavens

tugging at my wandering heart.

Galaxies form, emerge, and collide.

Supernovas explode.

While I squint and stare and point at the sky,

as far as my feeble eyes can perceive.

Wondering what these massive beings are.

How far away could they be?

Wondering how I fit into this cosmic realm.

How inconsequential I seem.

Twilight

Twilight pulls me from my deep reverie,

holding all of my secrets in the humid air.

But I won't fret over things that You're pondering,

because I know Your thoughts of me

float the wind as well.

And time might permit me

to hear every word You have spoken of me.

Still I know that we'll meet,

and share those things that we never thought to speak.

Maybe we'll float away on a distant ocean.

A Never-ending Hope

Comets soar and glide

while meteors somersault to the Earth.

Planets farther than my comprehension

spin ceaselessly,

never falling, never failing.

And we grasp to this land,

to this fortunate dirt,

adrift in the chaotic void,

blissfully unaware,

but filled with insatiable curiosity

with a never-ending hope of finding You there.

Grief

Blue Moon

Blue is the moon

under harsh evening light.

Drawn to the stars,

spreading frost through the night.

Casting shadows.

Casting flames.

Casting down the hope-filled dawn.

Replenishing the twilight.

Rejuvenating the darkness it spawned.

Bethany's Place

Bethany's bleeding

inside and out.

But the difference is negligible,

just as she.

Pour her heart out to those she loves,

but Bethany isn't the favored.

Bethany isn't the lovely one.

Tears falling and heart breaking,

Bethany pours her heart out.

She pours it out.

But she isn't speaking,

she isn't feeling,

she isn't breathing,

because she isn't the lovely one.

They Always Come

Set the trap and they follow.

They always follow.

Lure the prey and it comes.

It always comes.

There's always some.

They always come.

They always come.

Leave the door ajar.

They're not too far.

Leave the gate swinging.

Their curiosity will bring them.

There's always some.

They always come.

They always come.

Relate to their personal feelings-

it's the only way to start the healing,

the only one that understands them,

the only one that befriends them.

There's always some.

They always come.

They always come.

Fairy Tales

Fairy tales are breaking in,

and I know they're not good for my health.

Imagining and always wishing

is only lying to myself.

Cause when it all erases,

the watercolors drip from the faces.

The harsh reality lingers,

and the truth has begun.

Indulging into these things

would be nothing but an unwise decision.

Never lose my vision.

Never wander away.

I can't have all I want.

Foolish to try.

Imagining it can't help.

Then why do I try?

One Day

Someday it won't be there.

I will be free from this.

Someday I will.

I won't always be in fear.

I won't always have the pressure there,

the surmounting realization

of the finality of the situation,

the helplessness that comes

and the deep humiliation,

the degradation —

always there, always there.

One day it won't be there.

I will be free from this.

One day I will.

Eventuality

Seasons change.

People change-

the kindness of my heart

gone with the breeze of yesterday.

Burden of Pain

Like leaves changing hues in autumn dusk-

orange, brown, copper, and rust,

a shadow has rolled in

with the billow of dust.

And now the burden of pain

settles upon my brow,

as the fall storm cloud

banishes the summer drought.

As the Days Go On

Pounding pressure,

blinding flesh,

debilitating silver pain,

molding this mood.

Prayers abating,

hopeless, fading

under duress

of another power.

Still abrasive, evasive.

Can't pin me down.

My belligerent condition,

unyielding to submission.

Faulty wiring,

or careless handling,

pilfering all progress,

ignoring the presence of greatness.

Alone

Don't be so lonely;

better off alone.

Completely unsatisfied,

but isolation is the goal.

Break them off, break them all-

ties developed like chains

lingering, growing.

The imperative ending arrives

through blood and tears,

or through hope and encouragement,

but always alone.

Understand

Now I understand, I understand.

The bruises, the bleeding.

The crying, the pleading.

The wishing and waiting

for an invisible hand

to deliver me from

the hole I dwelled in.

But now I understand, I understand.

Looking for something that could never be.

Praying for things that weren't meant for me.

Fumbling in the midst of the dark

for a sign to show me

where I went wrong.

And now I understand, I understand.

The Breaking

Say it again,

more cavalierly this time.

And I'll wait by the door

with my churning insides.

Don't make it about me

when it's clearly your cost,

your troubles, your folly, your fall.

Just say the words again-

louder, and more clearly.

So there's no mistaking their intent or meaning,

their trajectory clear,

their landing solid, hitting their mark.

If you're going to be vocal

then do it with pride.

If you're going to be cruel

then also be wise.

Speak it with certainty

and annunciate your words.

Stand your ground,

no flinching – be firm.

Say those dreadful words

that can never be revoked,

and release me from this moment,

release me from this hope.

Something I Learned Today

You can be heartbroken

and grateful at the same time.

Love

Did You Know That You're a Star

Did you know that you're a star?

Shimmering, burning,

glowing throughout the night,

illuminating the skies.

Gas and flames circling through the dark,

shooting towards the earth,

carving a path of fire

through the chaos and dust.

You brighten this world

with a ferocious light.

A Love Song

I wanted to write a love song

but they always come out as poems.

And poorly versed ones at that.

The syntax is always wrong,

the metaphors contrite.

Disingenuous phrases born of inexperience.

Just pages of incoherent gibberish.

Upon further review,

maybe I can write a convincing pop song.

Moonlight Song

Sing me a song

from the moon to my heart.

The late evening hour

pulling me into the night,

adrift on a blanket of fog.

Won't you sing to my heart,

drawing me closer,

lulling me into slumber, into dark?

The moonlight beckons

and I follow in submission,

this unrequited love clawing at me.

Sing to my heart

and let it melt at your song.

Won't you whisper your love

through the night to the dawn?

Joy

Joy!

Unimaginable fulfilling joy,

joy at the sight of you.

What makes my day

and fills my night,

with pleasuresome and unforeseen delight.

Joy I feel in every way.

Seeing you I must convey.

Such joy at the sight of you.

Such joy at the thought of you.

Such joy I never knew.

Such unimaginable fulfilling depths

of joy for the love of you.

Brown Depths of Mystery

Your crystalline gaze

captures my eyes-

perfect brown depths of mystery.

Losing myself

in the miasma of your soul,

held hostage by the moment's intensity.

Pull me from the depths of loneliness and despair

and lock me in your arms of hope,

arms of future,

arms of trust.

Then promise me a world of dreams,

where your eyes forever hold me

in your gaze of love.

If I Were In Love

If I were in love
I would be shy.
Hide this heart
under an umbrella of denial
until the affections
culminated into an undeniable crush,
the sight of him making me blush.

And I'd work on myself
until I was sure he was pleased,
all the while demanding
he accept me as me.
If I were in love
all these things would turn around,
and seem so silly
in light of what I'd found.

Then I'd make a big spectacle
for everyone around-

angry then giddy then solemn then proud.

If I were in love

everyone would have no doubt

this passionate affair

was meant to come about.

He'd adore me

and I'd adore him.

The fun that we'd have

torturing each other

then making amends.

If I were in love

we'd fill our days up

with teasing and laughter,

with blissful endearments

and vows.

If I were in love

I'd build a life with him

Never worried about the past.

Looking forward to whatever

tomorrow would bring.

But every moment would be pressed

with doleful contentedness.

And every poem I wrote

would be about loving him.

Peace

Blessings

Warmest winter.

Constant blue tears.

Count my blessings

across the years.

The Eye of the Storm

Interlude.

Moment of peace and solitude.

Take this silence in my heart

to recuperate my mind.

Hold my peace, hold my tongue

and re-evaluate my time.

Sitting in the eye of the storm,

pacing through space,

waiting through time.

All this energy inside,

coiled and ready to strike.

Take this gift of solitude,

echoing through my thoughts

like a hollow cavern.

Take this day of peace,

and grow from the previous dark.

Take this day of rest,

and prepare for the gathering storm.

Dream Country

I don't need a peaceful tune

strumming me along,

or a thoughtful piece of prose,

reverberating through my mind,

silencing my own independent thoughts.

I don't need them inside.

Neither will a highly skilled academic help me

to convey my thoughts,

burn them into words,

melt them onto paper.

Though well-intentioned they may be,

a professional cannot persuade

my thoughts into any certain form.

When all is said and done

I need none of these things

that I believed were vital.

They only served to distract me

from the voice that lies within me,

and the truth has come undone-

I need not one.

Fate of Green

Emerald green.

I used to hate that color.

Bright shining memories of Oz,

attacking my vision at every turn.

This birthstone of May

was my symbol of beginning,

my tragedy of remembering.

Every green, every shade

was a dastardly fiend.

But then I awakened – then I dreamed.

Then I became accepting of this fate of green.

Fast Getaway

Temporary stranger;

shelter as I flee.

Summer stars

and summer cars.

Watch my getaway.

Responsibilities amiss.

Problems can wait.

How many hours of sadness and stress?

How many days of unrest?

Never matter for now.

Burn that speed limit

as stranger and I fly.

Melody

A gentle tune

strumming everywhere.

A magical world

of drums and guitars,

creating a melody

flowing straight from the heart.

All Over Winter

This is the time of my joy.

A time of cocoa nights

and Christmas lights-

a winter world in store.

This is the time of my innocence.

My memories are faded,

and my hopes are jaded,

but my winter dreams still exist.

This is the time of my life-

the time I hope will last,

the time I enjoy my past,

complete with a hymn to purify it.

Reflections

Maddening

Maddening.

It's maddening in here.

Times are wavering,

drying my spirit through.

Dry bones turned to dust,

ashes in the tombs.

This agony, this draught of life,

this penchant for aggravated death.

What impossible meaning of hope

do you choose?

The theft of my breath,

your words haunting my very soul.

It's mad to attempt these impossible goals,

but the sane have never been bold.

Human Behavior

People are strange,

stranger than me-

a novelty I can't believe.

Untold curiosity

that bleed through the pores,

through the eyes.

People are weird.

Mildly fascinating

with their little lives,

and their little families,

and their little things.

People are bizarre.

Such stories they lead.

Mysterious pasts

and peculiar presents.

They simply bewilder and confound me.

The Thirty Faces of Man

And then it begins-

when the day is long,

and the sun is worn

and no one is left to wander.

I will swoop down

with my wings of deceit,

and leave you to starve while I plunder.

Who shall betray the desires of man

and the feelings I must endure?

For I am the one who keeps the night

and light the sun rays with grandeur.

And when it begins-

once the fear is great,

and the hope is lost

and no one remembers his mother.

I will reveal myself

with my tattered scars,

and devour those left to smother.

You, with your ineptness and passivity,
dare to challenge my authority?
For I am the one who breathes the sea
and swallows the power with the majority.

And as it begins-
once the night is at large,
and the cells are unbarred,
and the guards are in their restless slumber,
my escape will be made,
my dream will parade,
and I'll trample those who put freedom asunder.

For I am the voice who guides the wise
in these halls of doom,
and I shall prevail in spite of these chains
that bind me to this room.

Things

Three years and life is over.

Three years of your cold shoulder.

Three years of dreams,

and I've lost three years it seems.

Three years of crying and of hoping no one sees.

It is time for me to let go of things.

Three years so hard,

and three times I was scarred.

Three ghosts that I wish I did not know,

and if you look the wounds may still show.

It is time for me to let go of things.

Old Maid

Someone once said I'd always be alone.

They called me an old maid.

Was there any cause for uncertainty

in my step?

Any moment to retrace my path?

Then I find a calling – set apart in an ugly world.

Without a doubt I choose to stare into

this sea – a mirror please.

Do not answer the door of this cold knocking wave.

Do not examine the spell on me.

Spinster

I do not spin,

nor web or weave.

I certainly do not loom.

Knitting is obscure to me.

I dare not crochet – shan't be my fate.

Straw to gold

would make a fortunate soul.

But I've no knack for dealing,

nor any machine to manage.

I could always forge along,

make do anyhow,

though I won't have craft work to show for.

A name will have to suffice somehow.

The Softest Song

One last word.

One verse.

One line.

No softer song

than the whispers of my heart,

breathing life onto the paper

one poem at a time.

To Take a Breath

There are so many poems inside me
still left to be written.
I feel them beating in my chest,
hear them gathering in my mind,
waiting to take a breath,
to be released into the night.
Words yearning for paper,
pressing forward toward the light,
interpreting the sacred
emotions trapped inside.

Poetic Flow

Twisting words into pieces,

into figures, into lines.

This poetic nature taking form,

guiding my life.

One year after the other,

stumbling and blind

through the corridors of emotions

and thoughts and opinions,

twisting and turning over inside my mind.

These words they form a gateway,

allow access to inside.

From my mind to the pen to the page to all life.

And this poetry flows

As though nature had designed,

breathing heart into the world,

breathing the world into my life.

The Words We Didn't Speak

The moments.

The silence.

The feelings in between.

The thoughts hanging in the air.

The stillness that breathes.

The vibrant pause.

The truth within the meaning.

The meaning within the poem.

These are the seconds

that string us along.

that hold us captive,

that haunt us when they're gone.

The memory of the moment

filled with the words we didn't speak.

About the Author

Pamela Brown is a former English teacher and a self-proclaimed bibliophile. Pamela is obsessed with the written word. She has been writing for as long as she can remember and completed her first novel at the age of 11. At the age of 12, Pamela began writing poetry and never looked back.

Follow Pamela on social media:

Twitter - @pnicolebrown1

Tumblr – theliteratelife.tumblr.com

Instagram – pamela.nicole.brown

www.ingramcontent.com/pod-product-compliance
Lightning Source LLC
Chambersburg PA
CBHW061337040426
42444CB00011B/2965